How I Set Up A Leading Care Consultancy

First print October 2021

978-1-4717-9524-4

Imprint: Lulu.com

CONTENTS

TESTIMONIAL

"Sam cares. Care is central to his DNA. So for Sam to share his experiences of setting up and running a leading care quality consultancy makes complete sense. Under his excellent guidance, the beauty of this book is that he has been there and done it. Start his journey here, learn along the way and finish feeling inspired."

– Duncan Lewis,
Communication Trainer

INTRODUCTION

This book, like most books, tells a story. More accurately, it tells the first part of a story. It's the story of how I went from a personal crisis – redundancy and having my mortgage offer withdrawn – to setting up and running a leading care quality consultancy.

It's intended to be the first book of a series, entitled *The Adventures of a Care Entrepreneur*, and will cover the first five years. That part, the beginning, is the part of the process I get asked about most. The scary part. The part where you go from having a set salary that arrives on a set day every month, to launching yourself into the great unknown.

What is now a nationwide network of care improvement associates and the first UK care consultancy to franchise successfully, began with me, on my own, sitting in my kitchen at a laptop. Of course, there has been some good fortune along the way, but hopefully there are parts of my experience that may be useful to others. In particular, I'm thinking of those involved in the care sector or who find themselves in the same position I did in 2017 – about to leave the relative safety of a job and taking the first, tentative steps across the choppy waters of self-employment.

I sometimes think of it like that, like crossing a fast-moving river. The first part is to be brave enough to step off the bank. After that, you're looking for stepping-stones, but the truth is that most of those stones won't appear until your foot is already in the air.

In so many ways, that first step is the most important.

Boldness has magic in it.

ACKNOWLEDGEMENTS

This book is dedicated to my wife, children and all my wonderful family and friends, who have continually inspired me, stood by me and supported me through the challenges along the way.

It is also dedicated to my valued business associates, colleagues and customers, who have been there and supported, inspired, mentored, encouraged and taught me. Their many (and sometimes harsh) lessons have been much appreciated.

Rachel Bryan
Fae Mell
Louie Werth
David Ruston
Charlotte Middleton
Hilary Spilsbury
Michael Prior
Barry Stanley Wilkinson
Jenn Crowther and 'Yorkshire in Business'
Tony Robinson OBE
Jonathan Copley
Anna Farmery

Paul Douglas
John Artley
David Noyes
Liam Palmer
Yvonne Hignell
Duncan Lewis
'Big Ian' Donaghy
Angela Fletcher
Karen Ritson
Salinder Sumra
Tina Boden
Julie Wright
Sarj Radia
Mat Whittingham
Cheryl White
Asquith & Co Accountants
Claire Artley

Thank you, I have been inspired by and learned from you all.

Me with our two younger kids

FOREWORD

by 'Big Ian' Donaghy

So many people tell you…
"Never expect YOU from others."
Sam Barrington is the exception to this rule – a diamond in a world of coal.

He has ambition but NOT for himself – for those around him.

He spots potential and ability in people and gives them the opportunity to shine in their own right, helping others to help others whilst he gets out of their way to let them do what they do best without interference.

THAT is his true skill.

Sam is driven not by money but by kindness and the impact that kindness brings to help people feel like they belong and can flourish.

He can be seen most days coming up with ideas, making his calls and walking by his beloved Scarborough beach.

This book is the starting pistol, NOT the finish line.

This is a 'work in progress' from a 'man at work' who throws everything into everything and who, despite being a busy man, ALWAYS makes time for others.

He has felt how it feels to be treated well and badly and is determined that no-one should encounter the latter in any care setting.

Sam is a well-respected and liked cheerleader for social care, an advocate for people without a voice but most importantly, an incredible dad.

This book is the 'once upon a time' that will lead to so many people being cared for enjoying a happier ever after.

Watch this space.

He's only just begun…

1

In 2017, I was doing pretty well. At 38, I was Head of Operations for a care consultancy company; it was a good, steady job, or so I thought. I had been in post for eight or nine months and was on a decent salary – a culmination of my 20 years' experience in the care sector.

This more senior, well-paid role tied in with other plans I had at home. My wife and I intended to leave our rental years behind and buy our own house for our growing family. That would involve fees, furnishing costs and getting a mortgage. You know, all that serious, grown-up stuff that seems to happen when you hit middle age. My job, of course, was central to this.

However, there was a small issue. A key element of my role was concerned with bringing in new business, but I found this very difficult. As one of only three consultants, the majority of my time was spent on the road, visiting care providers and actually carrying out consultancy work. In short, what I was doing can be summed up with a phrase that I've since heard so much that I think of it as a cliché, but I am going to use it anyway.

I was working in the business, rather than on the business.

My working day was so consumed with the nuts and bolts of the job that I had no time to strategize or do any 'big picture' stuff. I was only human, after all, and there were only so many hours in a day. My wife and I had a young son, and two older children between us. Outside of work, my time was also really at a premium.

Wanting to focus on a solution, I suggested to my boss that the company adopt an 'associates model'. We could partner with professionals to do the consultancy work for us, I thought, allowing senior employees like myself to be freed up to focus on the business. For her own reasons, she rejected the idea, which was her choice. It was her business, after all, and I guess it was not an approach she agreed with. Of course, I found that a little frustrating, but I enjoyed my job and was generally happy with where life was taking me, so I just got on with it.

At the same time, my wife and I found a small house that suited us. We took our kids to view it, and they loved it. They chose the rooms they wanted, the bank approved our mortgage application, and everything looked set.

If that had all panned out, you probably wouldn't be holding this book in your hands right now. But it didn't. Destiny had other ideas.

One morning, I received a phone call from my boss,

asking me to meet her at the office; an entirely routine thing, as far as I knew. I had just come off the back of a stint of training provision, delivering sessions to a local authority group of care providers. It had gone very well, and I received some lovely feedback from the attendees. I hoped, of course, that it might trigger some referrals or repeat bookings to bring in some extra business for the company.

I arrived back at the office and typed up my notes about the training on a computer, eager to relay the positive news to my boss. I hoped and believed she would share my optimism about where all this could lead. When she walked in, I looked up and smiled. There were only the two of us there.

"The session was fantastic," I told her. "All the attendees were so enthusiastic."

There was a brief pause, and I could tell by her flat facial expression that this meeting was not about that.

"Sam," she said, avoiding my eyes. "We're not going to continue with your role."

It was one of those moments where everything stops. I wasn't sure how to respond.

"Oh," I replied.

We had a great working relationship, and I could tell that saying this pained her. In fact, she ended up in tears, but the lack of new business had contributed to the outcome, even though I didn't feel that it was really my fault. I had a month on full pay to get my head together, but after that, I was out.

Naturally, there was a short period of, "Oh God, what am I going to do?" But in my case, that only lasted a few minutes. If there was going to be any chance of buying a home, I would need to make a new plan, and quickly.

After that meeting with my boss, I started that very day. I took that first step. I guess, to some degree, I was pushed. But I still took it.

I went home, spoke to my wife, and told her I was going to set up a business of my own. I had a mission and at that point, nothing to lose.

For a lot of people, the care sector and entrepreneurship are not necessarily an obvious combination. Care, after all, is not a money-focused industry, or at least it shouldn't be. It's a people-focused one.

Perhaps that's the key to a lot of this. I've always been a people person. But whatever the explanation, this combination of care and running my own business felt natural straight away. Maybe my upbringing and background had a part to play in that.

My son Jack made this Lego 'social care logo' during lockdown, at age 6. It's based on the care badge.

2

Growing up in York and then Scarborough, in the '80s and '90s, my mum, Jackie was a social worker and very proud of it. She always had jobs that involved improving the lives of young people or people with disabilities. My Dad, Rick, on the other hand, was quite different. He and Mum split up when I was little, but I used to spend time with him, my lovely step mum and my sister up in Teeside where they lived. My Dad had engineering inclinations and was into all sorts of things. He loved classic cars, for example, and would buy older cars, refurbish them, then sell them on at a profit. He constantly created new business ideas. Not all of them worked, but Dad was definitely an innovator; making his own way rather than taking a job and being on someone else's payroll. He sometimes spoke about it with me, about how much better it is to be your own boss and make your own decisions. "If you work for someone else," Dad would say, "your fate is always in their hands."

My grandparents also made a big impression on me as

a youngster. My paternal grandad ran a fish 'n' chip shop in Scarborough, while my maternal grandparents owned a clothes shop and, later, the first health food shop in the town.

The entrepreneurial spirit clearly ran in our family, although as a kid, I obviously would not have called it that. It was all just work as far as I was concerned, but I have no doubt now, looking back, that these things influenced me a great deal. Children learn by example, after all.

My stepfather, who moved in after Mum and Dad separated, was an excellent guitarist, so it was perhaps only natural that as a youngster, my biggest interest by far was music. I had bleached blonde hair, and I played the piano, guitar and wrote songs. I never had music lessons or concerned myself much with the technical side. I just played by ear and developed a feel for my instruments. I played in a three-piece grunge band, and like many teenagers, dreamed of headlining Glastonbury or going out on tour. In fact, I kept music going in one form or another right into my early 30s. I did achieve a little bit of success, playing festivals and even releasing a track on iTunes, but I think I always knew it would be tough to make a living at it.

At 17, I had an appointment with the school careers advisor. A Levels weren't working out for me, and I needed a new direction. I enjoyed the social side of sixth form and had a large group of friends, but sitting and concentrating for long periods did not suit me at all. I was a sociable type and much better at talking than writing. I suppose it's possible that these days, I may have been diagnosed with ADHD or something, but such things were not so well known back then. Mum attended the meeting with me, for support, and of course the advisor was a little cynical when he heard my plans for a career in music.

"It's very unlikely to work out for you," she told me, bluntly. "It hardly works out for anyone. You know that, don't you? Why don't you get involved in something a little more dependable and do your music on the side? That way you have an option if it doesn't work out."

It didn't sound like terrible advice, to be fair.

"How about the care sector?" she asked.

I thought about it, and it seemed a reasonable suggestion. I had always considered myself a caring person, had done voluntary work in the sector and enjoyed meeting new people. It seemed like a line of work that would allow me to use communication skills, which had always been a strength of mine. I reckoned there was the possibility for it to be quite a fun job.

I decided to follow the advice and started a National Vocational Qualification (NVQ) in care, which involved working in a small, two-site residential care provider for people with learning disabilities. One site was for people who needed full-time care, such as those with some complex physical disabilities, while the other site was for those who were more independent but still needed assistance and support to get through the day.

I loved how I got to do the things that the people I was helping were doing. Supporting somebody to go swimming meant that I got to go swimming too. Sometimes, I even took residents to the pub. I got to experience life with them and even became something like a friend. Of course, there were professional boundaries, but it's natural for human beings who spend a lot of time together to develop a bond.

One lovely individual, who we'll call Dave (not his real name), loved music, especially rock. I took him out to a local venue called The Jolly Roger, where my stepfather was playing with his band. It was fantastic to see how much Dave enjoyed the show. My personal connections with the band meant I was able to take him on stage to meet them all afterwards too, which really excited him. He collected autographs from the musicians and had the time of his life.

Overall, it felt like a thoroughly satisfying way to make a living. I was enabling the lives of others while having a great time myself. What more can you expect from a job?

Despite that, after finishing and gaining my NVQ, I left care briefly and went to work in a music shop in the middle of Scarborough. I guess I found it hard to shake off the music bug. It had been such a big part of my life for so long, and I think a part of me hoped that if I stayed as connected to the scene as possible, something could still happen. Within a year, though, I realised my heart was more in care. Perhaps I grew up a little. There was no real future working in a music store, so I found myself a job at a nearby independent care home.

The owner there was a former learning disabilities nurse and was extremely impressed with me, right from the get-go. My ability to relate to the clients caught her eye, and she urged me to build on my skills.

"You're so good with our residents," she said. "Why don't you think about doing a nursing degree?"

It felt like sensible advice, so after working there for a few months, I used my NVQ and GCSE qualifications to get onto a nursing course at Leicester De Montfort University.

My time in Leicester, from 1998 to 2001, was the most exciting three years of my life. The course was very vocational in structure, so we were assessed on the job, which suited me. We experienced hospital settings, mental health settings, settings for older people and for those with learning disabilities. It gave us a really solid grounding in all aspects of nursing and helped me to view the sector from various angles. While studying, I supplemented my income by setting up a little window cleaning round in Leicester, which went quite well. Even back then, there was something in me that was attracted to running my own business.

Throughout all my different student nursing placements, certain things really jumped out at me. It was the period when people with learning disabilities were still being assisted to move into community settings, following the Community Care Act of 1990. That meant that some learning disability care still took place in hospital type settings, and for one placement, I was sent to a ward turned over to that purpose. It's bizarre now to think that we used to house people with learning disabilities on a ward, that such an institutional setting was their *home*. A ward with eight beds – not really an appropriate place to be housing people, at all. I guess it was an indication of how that kind of care was in the past.

There were times when residents would need to be moved and staff would lift them from their beds onto a wheelchair, or vice versa, using very basic and rough manual handling techniques. I found this incredible. Located in the ward was a hoist, something which had been emphasised in our training. The correct way to move a person was by using this piece of equipment, but some of the staff preferred to manhandle those in their care, perhaps through habit. Even as a student nurse, I was very alert to these examples of bad practice. The risk of injury, either to staff or person, was obvious. All it needed was for a foot or a hand to slip and both the individual and nurse could hit the floor.

Another time, I was placed at a general nursing cottage hospital. An older lady staying there asked me for a glass of water.

"Of course, I'll get you a jug," I replied, and I went to the kitchen and came back with a jug of water and a glass.

The older lady was thrilled and incredibly grateful, which I found weird. It was only some water, after all. Later, one of the senior nurses took me to one side.

"What are you doing?" she asked. There was more than a touch of hostility to her tone.

"I'm just giving her some water."

"You shouldn't be doing that."

"Why? It doesn't say nil by mouth or anything on her notes. She was thirsty."

"Love," the nurse said. "If she has some, they'll all want some, won't they?"

I looked at her in bemusement.

"And then our whole shift," she went on, "will be a nightmare. We'll just be taking everyone to the toilet, non-stop."

I could not believe what I was hearing. The availability of water is a basic human right, and it's a nurse's job to take people to the toilet if they need it. As far as I was concerned, that sort of attitude had no place in nursing.

I thoroughly enjoyed my days as a student nurse, but I also learned some valuable lessons. It was clear to me, as I stood in my gown and mortarboard to proudly collect my certificate in 2001, that there were some areas of the sector that badly needed improvement. As I looked forward to my professional life, I knew that I would be championing person-centred care, care that was focused on the needs of the individual. Care that also involved the individual in the decision-making process.

I wanted to empower and enable people. To give them dignity. It was as simple as that.

Hometown of Scarborough

Me and two of my younger sisters as children

3

With university behind me, I remained in the Leicester area and found my first job in nursing, which was at a Secure Training Centre for young offenders. The provision was essentially a small prison for children aged 11 to 16, who were too young to go to a youth offending institution but were considered too risky to house in an open provision.

It was a challenging role, but one I enjoyed. A large chunk of my work involved patching kids up after a fight or when they had been restrained by a member of staff. I also had to administer medications to those on prescribed drugs – usually to treat some sort of mental health condition. Counselling also played a significant part, as I would talk the young people through any incidents they were involved in, which helped to build rapport. It was nice to be viewed as a trusted adult by them and someone they felt they could open up to.

I was the first person they met when they were inducted,

which I viewed as something of a privilege. After sentencing, they would be brought to us in a van, whereupon I would be called on to conduct a medical examination. I always made a point of making them feel welcome and settled. Sometimes, of course, the circumstances around their crimes could be quite unsettling, but I always tried to put that to one side. The sheer pointlessness of some of the violence was especially difficult to accept. One boy was brought to us after stabbing an American tourist.

"What did you stab him for?" I asked.

"I asked him for his camera, and he wouldn't give me it," the child replied in a matter-of-fact voice.

It was as simple as that, and that tourist was left in a critical condition. I always tried to frame things in my own mind by reminding myself that these were just children. They hadn't decided to commit these acts through free will. Life had dragged them in that direction. Most were from very difficult home situations and had suffered various kinds of trauma in their early lives. In many ways, they were as much victims as perpetrators.

However, after a year or so working there, I felt it was time for a new challenge and began actively looking for opportunities, checking job advertisements and so on. I saw one, which was for a deputy home care manager for a local company. The advertisement stipulated that they were only accepting applicants with a nursing qualification, although it looked like quite a challenging, more senior role that involved managing a number of people. I felt I was unlikely to get it, as I was still only 23 years old and relatively inexperienced in the sector, but decided it was worth a punt. In particular, I was quite attracted by the idea of leaving shift work behind. My STC job had made it difficult to spend any consistent time with my partner, as I often worked nights.

I was surprised to be invited to interview, where it was explained to me that the job entailed opening up a new homecare branch in the city, as the company, ENA Care, had just won a new contract. The provision would total 3,500 hours per week of home care spread over 120 service users with 60 staff. They wanted someone to oversee it all and to recruit a new team of care co-ordinators. At that stage, there was no office and nothing was really in place.

I turned up to the interview in a suit, as I thought that was appropriate for a managerial role. It went quite well, I felt, and I left the interview pleased that I had made a decent show of myself. I had no real expectations of getting the job, so was thoroughly surprised when the two interviewers called me the same day and offered it to me.

Of course, I accepted, but this was perhaps the first time in my life that imposter syndrome kicked in. The job carried a nice salary and came with a company car and credit card. It really felt like a huge jump for me. Although I was determined to do a good job, I didn't know if could, and that little voice of doubt at the back of my head made itself heard.

In truth, at the beginning, I wasn't a very good manager. I learnt on the job, and it was a steep learning curve. I realised very quickly that there was a lot more to this role than only caring about people. Of course, I had to keep that in mind, as care was the core purpose of my work, but my job was much more about leadership. That meant I had to adopt a positive mindset and strive to be someone that the staff could look up to – not easy when many of them were older and more experienced than I was. I had to earn people's respect by showing that I was serious and focused on doing a good job.

To begin with, our 'office' was a room set aside in one of the care homes that the company ran. The phones rang constantly and staff would come back to the office tired and upset. People often faced bereavements and other difficult situations on their shifts. I learned, through experience, how to cope with conflicts and problems. I think, in many ways, this was where I cut my teeth as a care entrepreneur. Of course, I wasn't an entrepreneur at the time, I was still on somebody else's payroll. But the skills I learned on that job at such an early age provided the foundation for what I would go on to do later.

I stayed in that role for a couple of years then moved on to various other jobs in the sector over the course of the next 15 years or so. During that period, I started another little side-line too – an organic veg delivery round. There was a company already doing this, but they weren't delivering to the area I lived in, so I contacted them and suggested they sub-contract out to me, which they agreed to. That was quite good fun and something I did to earn a few extra pounds at weekends.

I worked as a training manager for one company, then moved onto the local authority side of things, where I was a case manager and then a project manager for five years. After that, I returned to the private sector to work as a quality director, before moving into consultancy.

It was a move I was thoroughly enthusiastic about, and I felt, by this point in my life, that I had experienced the care sector from various sides and had a solid grounding in all of it. Having been a care worker and a manager of care workers, I understood both sides of the business.

4

Despite starting an exciting new job, 2014 was also a difficult year, as my dad was admitted to hospital for alcoholic liver failure. Alongside the stress of seeing a parent in such poor health, I found myself also questioning the quality of the care he received. Often, I had to challenge decisions that were being made by doctors, simply because Dad hadn't been included in those decisions. He was still compos mentis and had a right to be involved in discussions that could affect him.

For example, the doctors put 'do not resuscitate' in my dad's file and on a sign above his bed. Obviously, it was felt that the liver damage was so advanced that it was not worth reviving him if he went into cardiac arrest or something similar. To have something like that decided without having it discussed with you is a major infringement of human rights as far as I was concerned. It really upset Dad, too.

The whole thing was a big shock for all of us, especially Dad. "That's it," he said, "I'm never touching a drop again."

To be fair, he didn't either, but sadly, the diagnosis had arrived too late. We asked about the possibility of a liver transplant but were told he wouldn't survive it.

As Dad's condition became more advanced, he was moved into a nursing home, which was a really big deal for us. Dad was only 60 and, as far as we knew, was only a social drinker. Of course, it emerged later that he had been drinking heavily on his own, often after everyone went to bed. Nonetheless, he was no age to be nearing the end of his life. My youngest son had only just been born, and I was faced with the realisation that they would never know each other.

Beyond all the difficult feelings, two things really struck me from the experience with my dad. Firstly, the patient really needs to be included in any decisions made about their care. Even if these conversations are potentially difficult, competent professionals should be able to handle them sensitively. Otherwise, the patient will be left feeling powerless and ignored.

The other lesson I learned was to do with end of life and how that can play out. Dad's condition deteriorated to the point that he was unconscious most of the time, but one night, just before Christmas 2014, he suddenly perked up. He was awake for nearly the whole evening, making conversation and cracking jokes. We put some Christmas music on and watched the movie *Home Alone*. I remember that at one point in the evening, Dad gave me a big grin and said, "You thought I was a goner, right? You thought you'd got rid of me, didn't you?" It was just like having the old Dad back, and we were all in great spirits.

The next day, Dad passed away. That evening had been his last. Of course, there was grief, but there was also a sense of good fortune, as we had been able to spend one last happy night together. That taught me a lot about how important it is to have family members included as closely as possible in somebody's last days and hours.

Obviously, Dad's illness and eventual death, along with the birth of my son, exerted a fair amount of pressure over our wellbeing and personal life. This was then added to further down the line when I was made redundant, which brings us back to where this book began.

It was April 2017. My wife was in work at the time and at that point I had a month's pay to tide me over, so the redundancy wasn't quite the end of the world, although it was obviously a blow. Before long, the bank noticed that my salary payments were not appearing in my account anymore and withdrew their mortgage offer. This was disappointing for all of us and meant we had to stay in our rented house for the time being.

I think, in some ways, these things just made me even more determined. I reckoned I had some decent ideas, and that if I could put them into action, I would be able to create something capable of making a living.

My vision was to establish a business according to the

suggestion I had made to my ex-boss. I would re-engineer what I had seen working in my previous role so that I would be able to work on the business, rather than in it.

Starting Out

Some people may laugh at you when you are the only person in your new start-up company, and call yourself 'Founder & CEO' or something similar.

They will say,
- "You are the only officer in your company, never mind the Chief Executive Officer."
- I've seen posts on this very subject on LinkedIn.
- Some will criticise people like you, some will hate on you.
- Let them laugh, keep going, call yourself what you like, aim high, evolve and stick with your vision.

I've found this:

- There is far more love and support out there than there is hate.
- You won't always be a start-up...
- and you won't always be the only person in your company if you don't want to be.

My plan was to sub-contract the consultancy work to associates. The difference between the fees I received from care providers and the day rates I paid associates for their work would be my margin. I knew I would need to get the right people who would be willing to work for the right rate and of course I would need to find the clients, but I was sure it could work. The margin on each individual assignment would not always be very much, but if I could grow my vision into a large team of consultants, working over a wide area, maybe even the whole country, it would scale up into a nice net profit.

In the first instance, I would need a company name. My wife and I brainstormed ideas and for some reason settled on 'the Care Improvement Audit Group'. I used GoDaddy to create my own website that very evening and bought the domain name *theciagroup.co.uk*. I went on Fiver.com and paid someone a fiver to design me a logo. Then I found another online service and ordered some business cards. That was it. I had started. My start-up costs were no more than a couple of hundred pounds.

The next morning, I got up with my wife and put the jacket on that I used to wear into the office in my old job. Of course, I could have sat around in my pyjamas if I'd wanted to, but I wanted this to feel right, as much as anything. We had a coffee together and then my wife left to go to work.

"I need to get to work too," I told her.

She smiled. "Good luck!"

"I'm a CEO!" I replied.

Just by saying it, it felt real.

Almost straight away, the company name attracted attention. It became a talking point. Obviously, the acronym CIA is well known around the world for other things, but I liked that. If it got people talking, that was a positive.

After a couple of weeks, I realised that the full name was too long and unwieldy. I would need something snappier, but I was determined to keep the CIA connection. I racked my brains and at last came up with 'Care Improvement Associates'. The very first time I said it out loud, something about it just felt right.

Of course, at this stage, I was entirely a one-man band. The vision for a network of associates would come in time, I hoped, but in those early days, I would have to conduct any consultancy work I picked up myself. Nonetheless, I hoped some work would come in as soon as possible, just to make it all feel real.

While waiting for my first client to come along, I found it quite hard not to check the job ads. It was tempting to apply for something, to maybe pick up another salaried position so that I had that security. But something always stuck in my head. My former boss, the one who made me redundant, was a fantastic person who mentored me a great deal. While we worked together, we often used to talk about this sort of thing, and she gave her insights into what was needed to succeed in business.

"Burn your boats," was something she always said. "If you give yourself a lifeline, you'll be too tempted to grab it. You need to put yourself in a sink or swim situation."

I repeated that wisdom to myself, sometimes several times a day. I had to, because in those early days I often woke up feeling very anxious.

"What are you doing?" I would say to myself. "You've got bills to pay, kids depending on you. You've got no money coming in!"

There were mornings where I almost caved in. "Who are you to go into business on your own?" I would think. It's what people refer to as 'imposter syndrome'. The truth is I was as well positioned as anybody to start a business like this, but it's easy to say that now, in retrospect. At the time, there were days when the whole thing was very psychologically challenging. That inner voice, I learned, that doubting Thomas that lives inside all of us, can really break you down. I had to consciously ignore it, really make a point of shutting it out. Stubbornly, I managed to stick to my guns, and by doing that, I avoided the easy lure of falling back into employment.

Everybody needs a bit of luck, especially at the beginning, don't let anyone tell you otherwise. And I certainly had a bit of that. I received a message on LinkedIn from one of the attendees at the training I ran in my previous job. Essentially, they were running a care home for people with learning disabilities and were really struggling. The Care Quality Commission (CQC) had down rated them on a recent inspection. As a result, they were losing pots of money and finding it very hard to gain new residents. No- one wants to place their loved ones in a failing care home, do they? This company needed someone to come on board for six months to help them turn things around.

If I was honest with myself, it wasn't the sort of contract I had hoped to win. My vision for CIA was to work with good providers to help them achieve an 'outstanding' rating in their CQC inspections. That's what drove me on, as an individual, to help as many companies provide outstanding care as possible. What a fantastic way to meet the needs of service users that would be!

This job, however, was something else. A company that was failing in its basic duties and needed help just to become compliant – it was literally the other end of the scale. Of course, I put all those thoughts to one side. CIA had to get up and running as a functioning consultancy. Maybe in the future, I would be fortunate enough to be selective about the clients I took on, but not while hunting for my first contract! I felt had to take whatever was offered.

The client offered me a £2000 a month retainer for working a couple of days a week, which in my position as newly self-employed, was a fantastic deal. It meant driving from my home in Driffield to Northampton two days a week; they were long days, but the money was enough to keep me ticking over in terms of paying the rent and bills. Most importantly, the time demands were light enough for me to continue growing my business the rest of the week.

In truth, that first contract turned into a bit of a nightmare. You could tell, as soon as you walked in, that it was terrible in nearly every way: there was a moody, bad-tempered atmosphere, it was dirty, it smelled awful, and the residents looked scruffy and unkempt, not to say bored out of their minds. There was no way anyone looking for a placement for their relative would choose it.

I carried out audits and gave them all sorts of advice, structured into a 'Quality Strategy', most of which they totally ignored. Their biggest problem was in meeting the guidance contained in the 2005 Mental Capacity Act centred around promoting independent decision making, dignity and choice. I kept telling them that they needed to put their residents and their staff first. It has always been a core belief of mine that if people are happy in a care setting, it creates a successful environment. They didn't seem to understand that perspective. As far as the owners of that care home were concerned, everything was about finance.

"We can't invest because we're not attracting any residents," they would say.

"You're not going to get any residents unless you invest!" I would reply.

It felt like banging my head against a brick wall, but CIA was up and running.

First office

Second office

Newest office, 2019

Newest office, 2019

5

As a care consultancy, I was very aware of not having a shop window. When my grandparents ran their clothes store, years before, it worked on the same basis as any other shop. People would walk past, look in the window and see what was on offer. If they liked what they saw, they might stop and go inside. Some of those people might then actually buy something, but it all started with that shop window and what was displayed in it.

The way that I came to think of it was that my website and, to a large degree, my presence on LinkedIn were my 'shop window'. This was where people would find information about me and my company, see what I was all about and connect with me. The strength of that connection might then determine whether we ever worked together.

In many ways, my LinkedIn journey was the same as my business journey. As my presence and number of connections on the site increased, my business expanded. I first set up a profile while working in my previous job. It was one of the things my old boss mentored me about.

"You need to get 500 connections," she told me. "Then it can become a useful tool. Before that, you're wasting your time."

Dealing with critics

You will find that some people criticise you for taking risks and making mistakes when you are starting or scaling a business.

Just remember that you are the one actually doing it, while the ones criticising you are often the ones sitting on the side-lines, not doing it and not taking any risks.

"You don't have to be great to start,
but you have to start to be great,"

– Zig Ziglar

I made the effort, right from the beginning, to project a highly professional image online. I didn't tell anyone that the business was only me, on my crappy old laptop in my kitchen, or that my laptop was as slow as anything and even had a couple of keys missing – no one needed to know that. In the eyes of the world, Care Improvement Associates was a company, not a one-man band with serious tech issues. I really believed that one day I would have a big team of consultants working with me, maybe some employees too, and that the 'CEO' tag would be justified.

Very soon, I had built up a network of connections,

which has steadily grown ever since. Many of those early connections are people I have gone on to do business with and some have even become good friends. It is from this foundation, that CIA went on to become such a success.

In the end, I terminated that first contract from my side. The company were very poor, in my opinion, were not really implementing any of my recommendations, and as a result were failing to improve. It wasn't really the sort of provider I wanted to be associated with and certainly not the corner of the market in which I wanted to position my business.

The decision was helped by the fact that I got my first associate on board. Hilary joined me just three months after I set the company up, having been someone I worked with before on the local authority side. Hilary's involvement came about through a previous role. I contacted her and asked if she fancied being one of our associates. In the first instance, I didn't tell her that she would be the only one, although that became apparent quite quickly. We met up, had a meeting of minds over coffee and I was delighted that she chose to take up my offer.

Hilary was very experienced as a care inspector and knew all the regulatory details inside out. I was very lucky to have her, and she was absolutely fantastic from day one. Her first job for me was to go out to this failing care provider and conduct a mock inspection. I knew that her familiarity with CQC criteria would lead to a very thorough and professional report. Predictably, when her conclusions came through, they were pretty damning. I conferred with Hilary, then telephoned the client.

"Look," I said, "we've done everything we can do for you. You have our recommendations. Whether you choose to implement them or not is up to you."

That was that. Contract, over. It had been useful to me as a jump-start for the company, but if I am honest, I was glad to see the back of them. I felt that any sort of long-term association with them would be damaging to my business's reputation and would prevent me from going where I wanted to go.

When I look back now, I think this is something else worth emphasising. It's important to have a vision for your business and to try to stay true to that vision. It would have been very easy to keep that contract going and to keep taking the £2000 a month. At that stage, that could even have been viewed as the sensible thing to do, but in my bones, I felt that the contract wasn't right for the company, so I made the difficult decision to end it.

During the whole three months I worked with that failing provider, I networked constantly, primarily through LinkedIn but also on the phone.

LinkedIn Tips

- You don't need to start your LinkedIn post apologetically with, "I don't normally post personal things on LinkedIn, but..."
- If it's something that you feel is relevant to you and your life, or even part of your personality, then it's part of you, and you are a key part of your business or work.
- I am happy to know about who you are as a person and what your story is.
- LinkedIn is no longer just a platform to show off your CV, recruit, be recruited or talk about 'professional' issues.
- You are your CV.
- You are your brand.
- It's a platform to network, get to know people and show who you are.

I'll be honest, I recruit, use suppliers and form associations with people and companies that share the same ethics and values.
   ...and if I'm really honest, those who I actually like as people.

Then, five months after starting the business, I found an office in a village outside town. It cost £200 a month for a tiny box room with a desk, window and filing cabinet. Nonetheless, this felt like an important moment. Care Improvement Associates was no longer operating from my kitchen table. We had an official headquarters. I posted about it proudly on LinkedIn, talking about my feelings of excitement.

In return, I got a few negative responses from people who felt LinkedIn wasn't for sharing personal views and insights.

"This site is for professional networking," they would say. "Go and post this on Facebook."

"But this is my work," I would reply.

Fortunately, I got much more positive feedback than negative. Many people actually told me the reason I was doing so well on LinkedIn was because I wasn't afraid to personalise it. Up to then, a lot of content that appeared on there could be quite dry and sterile. Other users connected with my approach. 'People do business with people'; that's another cliché, but one I believe in very much. I am sure that the way I presented myself on LinkedIn – as a real human being, on a journey with ups and downs – was a major boost to the development of the company.

Before long, I had five associates. They all came from either my own personal contacts or through Hilary. I found that after that, it was like I reached a kind of tipping point. With a small team already assembled and the company's reputation growing online, people began to approach me. I started getting messages from consultants who were looking for work and needed someone to find it for them.

Freelance consultants all had exactly the same problems I had. They had broken out on their own, leaving the safety net of a job behind, and needed to earn. All of them had the same concern – where to get their first contract. For that reason, they connected very easily with the personal journey I related on LinkedIn.

I knew from that point on that my business was going to

work. These people were experts in their field; experienced consultants who knew their stuff inside out, just like Hilary. What they weren't necessarily up for was marketing themselves – but that was my strength. I didn't have their knowledge or capabilities, but I had a knack for networking. That meant all those people and I were ideally suited to working together. They could do what they were good at and so could I. We could all provide what the other needed.

Of course, that meant I had to hold up my end of the deal and get work for these people, but I did not see that as a problem. I picked up the phone and rang as many care organisations as I could.

"Have you thought about having a mock inspection or having audits done to help you prepare for CQC?" I would ask. "It would really benefit you to have an independent report compiled so you can see where you stand."

Having learned my lesson from the first contract, I specifically targeted 'good' providers. I knew from my own background that most care providers were rated as good by the CQC. They weren't 'inadequate', they didn't 'require improvement' and they weren't 'outstanding'; they were 'good'. But what did the owners and management of good care providers have in common? Easy – they all wanted to be 'outstanding'.

What a fantastic thing for the people they support, but also to be able to put on your sales and promotional materials: "Our care is rated 'outstanding' by the CQC."

In my guts, I knew we could get business like this and that the market out there was potentially very big. This approach also helped to give Care Improvement Associates a unique identity, a USP (Unique Selling Point), to coin another overused term. All the other consultancies out there were consistently talking about 'CQC compliance'. I didn't want to do that, because as far as I was concerned, that would be selling ourselves short. Good providers were already compliant. They knew what needed to be done to be compliant because they were already doing it. What they needed help with was in taking that extra step to not just be compliant, but to be 'outstanding'.

On LinkedIn, the website and everywhere else, I steered the conversation away from being compliant and positioned Care Improvement Associates as a Care Quality Consultancy. I coined the phrase 'Be Outstanding' and used it a lot. Over time, this evolved into 'Let's Aim for Outstanding Together', which is now our company slogan.

This way of approaching things soon bore fruit. I picked up a couple of new contracts very quickly, including one with a massive care provider. I called them because I saw they were advertising to recruit a quality manager to work across all 40 of their homecare branches. I got through to one of their senior directors who worked on that side of the business and suggested that rather than recruiting someone to cover that internally, they would be better served by working with our team. We could go in on an independent basis and give them a really objective view.

The director listened to my pitch keenly.

"You know what?" he said, when I had finished. "That's a really good idea."

I went for a meeting at their head office. They wanted to know how many associates I had and what sort of coverage I could provide. The conversation went fantastically well and resulted in CIA winning the contract. That was such a big deal for us, as it meant that all 40 of their branches would need to be audited, and the contract would last for a year. It was still only five or six months since I started the business, and CIA was flying.

My entrepreneurial inspiration, my wonderful grandparents (a.k.a. La La's).

6

The big contract gave the company a lovely cash injection because I worked on an advance payment model. Other contracts followed, and within our first year of operation, Care Improvement Associates was more successful than I had really thought possible.

During follow-ups with clients, I always made a point of asking for testimonials. If they gave positive feedback, I would immediately ask if we could use what they said on our website or marketing materials. This is what drove the continual inflow of business. Connections on LinkedIn saw the steady accumulation of testimonials, which encouraged them to approach me to request our services.

We started to expand the services we offered too, providing training as well as audits and inspections. Our pool of contacts grew and grew, and by the end of our first year, I had 5000 connections on LinkedIn; 10 times more than when I started. I was able to move to bigger offices in my hometown of Scarborough, and it felt like the business was starting to go places.

Work / Life Balance

- Sometimes, 'being Dad' is what being a business owner looks like.
- Damn proud of this fact too.
- Yes, juggling the demands of a scaling business and school summer holidays (often in the rain) is tricky.
- Yes, you sometimes get emails and LinkedIn messages from people who are frustrated that you have not come back to them yet.
- Yes, you sometimes drop a plate or two when spinning six of them.
- Yes, it's harder to support your team if you're focusing on being a dad.
- But it's made much, much easier when you believe in and trust your amazing autonomous team and your team get what you are about.
- I didn't build a business model to get me richer in money,
- I built a business model that enables me to be richer in time, before the little ones think it's no longer cool to hang out with Dad.

Most importantly, for me at least, the business worked out in exactly the way I had hoped. The associate consultant model meant I was able to work on the business, not in it. It also freed up my time in other ways. Not having to commit to constant road-trips to visit clients meant I was able to spend quality time with my family – something that was incredibly important to me. I know that many small business owners find their work completely all-consuming, but I had designed this from the beginning to provide me with a nice work-life balance and that's what it was doing. I enjoyed the opportunity of being a part of my kids' lives, to be a proper dad. After all, that's what life's really all about, isn't it?

After our first year of trading, I also received notification that I had been nominated for the Hull and East Yorkshire Chamber of Commerce Business Person of the Year Award, 2018. It was a 'Dragon's Den' type situation, in which I had to talk through my business model and my accounts before a panel of judges. I was forced to go into great detail over figures, which have never been my strong point.

I was surprised to be shortlisted and invited to the awards night at Bridlington Spa, a beautiful local venue overlooking the sea, in which many major events are hosted. My wife and many of my friends came along to support me. I felt a little like an actor at the Oscars and to be honest, a bit of a fraud. The other finalists in my category all seemed far more established than me. They played little videos of each of us at work on a big screen. Mine was simply me in my office walking around then pretending to write something on my laptop, which my little gang of supporters found hilarious. Then they started to make the announcements and I prepared myself to smile politely and clap when the winner was declared.

"And the 2018 Chamber of Commerce Businessperson of the year," the MC said. Everyone went quiet. "Sam Barrington!" I literally could not believe it. All my party went mad, and I went up to receive the award. It was a fantastic night and a great personal validation for everything I had done.

A few reflections

I remember a few years ago...

I was informally offered a good chunk of money for Care Improvement Associates (CIA) theciagroup.co.uk
and a very attractive six-figure package.

That was a lot of money to me then and still is!

However, due to various reasons, (namely the hesitation in my gut, but also not really being the right person for the potential position on offer), it didn't go ahead.

It just goes to show, it's not all about money. It's about how something makes you feel.

It's got to be right for both parties.

You can't fit a square peg in a round hole (as they say).

Once you have tasted the freedom of running your own business, it's hard to go back to employment, unless it's absolutely right.

Trust that feeling!

One thing that I will always remember is the people who advised me to stick with growing CIA myself.

Thank you to you. You know who you are.

Also, thank you to the company, who were honest with me after a few discussions and who knew my heart wasn't in it and that it likely wouldn't be a good fit for me personally.

I'm still in touch with them now.

In hindsight, I'm so glad that job didn't work out!

I've happily continued to be 'unemployable' ever since!

With the business hitting its stride and growing rapidly, I decided to focus very clearly on the business culture I wanted to create. Central to that was our focus on 'Care Quality'. I wanted us to be a company that contributed to people in care receiving the best care possible. I tried to think of ways I could really firm that up, and through LinkedIn, I came across a guy called Louie Werth. Louie was doing a PhD and ran his own company called Care Research.

 I arranged to meet Louie in York, where we bounced ideas around over a couple of coffees. I told him I wanted to commission a piece of research that would identify the common denominators in care providers that get rated as 'outstanding'. In the homecare sector, as an example, I knew that only 1% of providers achieved that rating. What was it, specifically, that 1% were doing and all the others were not? That's what I wanted to know.

Guided by Louie's company, we then looked at every single provider in the country that had been rated 'outstanding' and sought out all the commonalities between them. It turned out there were 114 focus points that differentiated those companies from those who achieved lower ratings.

Many of these focus points were very simple to implement. Things like sending out satisfaction surveys and involving the people they care for and their families in the provision. Similarly, outstanding providers did the same thing with their staff teams, seeking out feedback on their experiences in the job and looking for ways to make employees' time at work more rewarding. They would then correlate all this feedback into a statistical report that could be used as a measure of how well they were doing from the point of view of those being cared for and those caring for them. This report could then be fed into an action plan, in a continual, annual cycle of service improvement.

The above is just one example – I won't list any more, as that actually turned into a book on its own. What's important to note is that this research was massively important to us as a business. It really helped us to drill down into the core of our company's mission, which was to 'aim for outstanding together'. We were able to present clients with a series of research-backed recommendations that were proven on a national scale. Off the back of this research, Bluebird Care, a massive, national home care company with headquarters in South East England, invited us to deliver research based masterclasses across their franchise network.

Something else that became apparent during this process was that the vast majority of the care sector still operated in very old fashioned, paper-based ways. They would gather evidence to show to inspectors and keep it in box files in an office somewhere. It was quite common for the head office of a care provider to have several shelves of these files, which all needed to be ordered and updated. It occurred to me that if a digital system could be devised for this purpose, it could potentially be a winning idea. This was something I would return to a little later.

In addition to the outcomes of the business, the culture I wanted to create was also about what it was like to work for us. It was important to me to make CIA people centred and family centred. One of my main motivations in creating the company was to be able to structure my days in a way that suited me, so that I also had time for life outside work. I wanted exactly the same thing for my employees.

Things reached a point, during 2019, that I knew I needed more help in the office. Both our client list and team of associates had grown considerably, and I was able to implement another part of my original vision. I always knew, without sounding big-headed, that my biggest ability was in networking and marketing. Whether that took place online or face-to-face, I had always been pretty good at dealing with other people. But to run and grow a business, you cannot just rely on that. You need to handle the financial side and the operational side as well.

With CIA becoming a national-level operator, working with huge clients like Bluebird, Cera and Voyage, I advertised for a manager. I was conscious that I would no longer be able to maintain the necessary quality on my own. Applications came flooding in, and I was able to choose someone who lived locally and could join me at our office in Scarborough. My new manager, Megan, made a significant impact.

To have someone working with me, not as a collaborator, like Louie, or an associate, like Hilary, but a full-time salaried employee, felt like another huge step. Just two years before, I had been working at the kitchen table with a shoddy old laptop, but now I was in a position to not only support myself, but to pay someone else a wage. It was a great move and a starting point for a new development of the company. Having a manager to come in to lend their time to parts of the business I needed help with really pushed things on.

Like most things though, it wasn't all plain sailing. Following a period of sustained success, I was about to enter a time of challenges. The first of these was during the late summer of 2019, when my stepson was diagnosed with a serious and aggressive brain tumour. This was an extremely stressful time for the family. By then, my wife was also an independent business person, running her own café. We both needed to support my stepson, but also both needed to keep our businesses going.

We went into survival mode and were forced to put business on hold as much as possible. It was a huge help to me that the office manager was able to hold the fort to some extent. The months that my stepson was in treatment actually reinforced to me what a great move going into business was. How stepping off the bank into the river two years earlier had been the right thing to do. In many ways, I had so much more flexibility than if I had been an employee somewhere. In that scenario, I would have been asking for time off and reliant on the goodwill of my employer.

Fortunately, my stepson has been making a good recovery. He is certainly the bravest person I have ever met. I have nothing but absolute admiration for him. By early 2020, it looked like the difficult times were easing a little. Of course, world events would prove that to be untrue.

When coronavirus struck in the first part of 2020, and the country locked down at the end of March, it was a terrible blow for the care sector and also for CIA. Much of our business was based around sending consultants out to work in care homes and other settings. Restrictions meant that was no longer possible. What on earth could we do?

It was another one of those moments when the doubting Thomas inside my head spoke up again. "You're going to need to pack this in and find a job," he said. "Your business won't survive this."

However, something that followed on from my previous work with Louie Werth gave me grounds for optimism. I had met a friend John, who was a software developer and whose son went to the same primary school as mine. We had worked together to develop ideas for an app. The idea was similar to that which I had discussed with Louie; a system that would enable care providers to digitally store all the evidence of outstanding care needed to showcase excellent care quality at inspections. It was conceived to be both a storage and guidance facility, providing hints and tips to users along the way. This led to the 2020 launch of another venture - Be Outstanding Ltd. An award winning care quality software, which not only proved a great success as a project, but also kept us in the minds of potential clients. Be Outstanding aligns perfectly with CIA and helped to establish us as a leader in our sector. Not only that, but it helped us plug the gap created by Covid, enabling us to support care providers remotely.

With a period of sustained success behind us, I felt it was time to take the next step. In Summer 2020 I met Rachel Bryan who I recruited after she had been made redundant from a senior role in the care sector. Rachel went on to become our Chief Operating Officer, (now as I write this, she has been promoted to our CEO). Then in spring 2021 we both head hunted a very talented Business Development Director, Fae Mell. They are a dynamic duo! An awesome team if ever there was one! Since then, CIA has become the first in the UK to franchise the care quality consultancy business model. I had received many enquiries, through LinkedIn and the website, asking how I achieved my success. It had often been suggested to me by Care Management Author and Friend, Liam Palmer, to run a conference or a workshop, at which I could provide a breakdown to attendees of how to go freelance, become consultants or run their own businesses. That idea was a great one, but never particularly appealed to me. Despite my music background, I am not a natural showman and couldn't see myself up on stage performing and motivating a hall full of people. I'm not really that kind of guy.

However, I am more than happy to be the face of my business online, or to talk with people one to one or in small groups. The idea of franchising came about after a conversation with a client. They ran a home care company that had been franchised and recommended that approach to me. The more I thought about it, the more it seemed a natural path to go down. Through that, we would train and mentor care consultants or those wanting to make the leap, who could then use our systems and branding to create their own stories and to build their own businesses.

We devised a model whereby franchisees receive the whole package: marketing, business development and finance, networking, CQC training, care quality audit training, market research, care research and, of course, the Be Outstanding software. As the Care Improvement Associates brand was now well respected by people working in the sector, interest was immediate. By the time this book was being written we were receiving as many as ten enquiries a week from potential franchisees. London East and Birmingham/Coventry franchise owners have both already come on board, with Devon and Cornwall joining us in coming weeks.

Care Improvement Associates is now a national-level company, with over 1000 assignments carried out through 500 care providers and with a nationwide network of approved associates on the books. We have three franchise branches in addition to our main headquarters in Yorkshire and the future looks bright. As I say, I now employ a full-time office team, and I'm very proud that I've managed to create a company in the way I always wanted. At Care Improvement Associates, we pride ourselves on offering four key benefits to our employees. Firstly, no set hours. Our employees manage their own diary. We measure success based on employee wellbeing, quality of service and positive business outcomes, not on counting the input of hours. Secondly, holidays are not limited to only four weeks a year as they are in most other jobs. Breaks are booked on a fair usage basis. People often tell me I'm crazy when they hear about this. They assume employees will take advantage and book endless holidays. This is absolutely not the case. When people feel trusted, they behave in a trustworthy way.

Thirdly, we run a family-first policy. This means the rest of us cover if an employee needs to care for a family member, take a relative to an appointment or pick up their children from school. They fit their work around their family commitments, not the other way around.

Last but not least, we are introducing a well-being package – not just for the rainy days, but in a proactive way. A qualified well-being coach is on hand to help with practicing wellbeing techniques, focused on promoting good mental health, stress prevention and managing any fear and anxiety.

Care Improvement Associates is therefore a company I'm extremely proud to have founded. Yes, we do okay financially, but that does not define us. We're something a little bit more than that.

Looking back...

- It's 25 years ago this year that I began as a trainee support worker earning £35 a week.
- It's 23 years ago that I started my nurse training on a £4500 per annum student bursary, working three jobs around clinical nursing placements and studies to top up my income as a window cleaner, bar man and care worker.
- It's 19 years ago that I started my first home care management role in the adult social care sector, managing a team of 60 care workers, delivering 3500 hours of home care per week.
- It's six years ago that I walked away from a toxic culture in a home care company where I was an underpaid and undervalued care quality and training director across a multi setting care group. Leaving was the best thing I ever did.
- Since then, I gained experience as an independent care quality consultant, was made redundant four and a half years ago.
- So, then I set up a nationwide network of care improvement associates, employed a wonderful senior head office team and co-founded an award-winning care quality software.
- Both trusted by national leading care brands.
- This month we started franchising our model and have found two franchisees (London and Birmingham),in a few weeks and are now building a million-pound business.
- Failure is not failure, it is experience. Harness it, use it, and it will drive you on.

Receiving Business Person of the Year Award 2018

We won the Innovation and Enterprise Award for our Be Outstanding Software

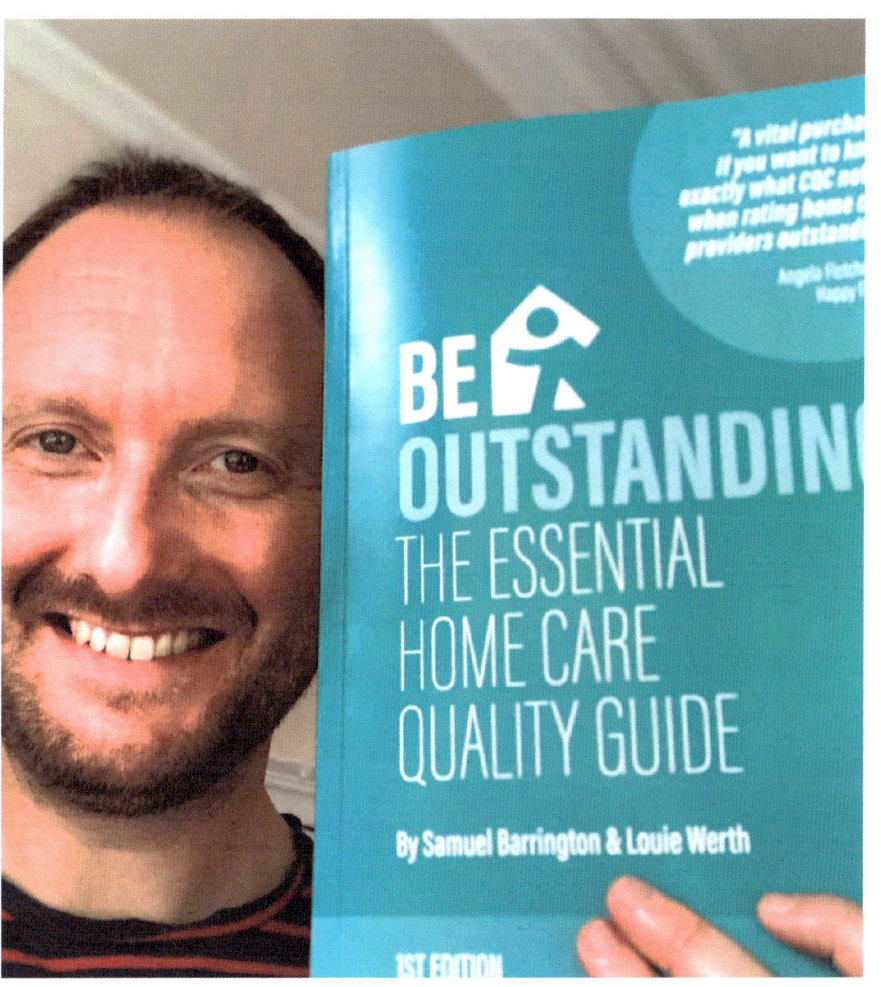

My first book with Louie Werth. 'Be Outstanding' The Essential Home Care Quality Guide.

Author Liam Palmer visiting to interview me.

Dave and I at the premier of BBC comedy, Scarborough.

Charity Ball with friends and colleagues David and Charlotte Ruston.

AND FINALLY

I'd like to leave the readers of this book with my top ten tips. These are the most important things to do or things that need to be avoided, in my experience. Hopefully, you can apply what's relevant to your own situation:

1. Don't compare yourself to others. You are on a different journey. Each journey is unique, and challenges are different. Everybody has different circumstances and various commitments going on in their lives that can cause things to move both forwards and sometimes backwards. Go at your own pace.

2. Look after your health and well-being first as a priority. Without that, you will have no business. That doesn't mean you have to be a gym fanatic, just whatever works for you. It may be a stroll, a swim, or something completely different.

3. Diary in a 'meeting' just to benefit you each day. I got this tip from author, speaker and musician, Big Ian. Personally, I do my best thinking and creating when walking or running alone, plus I get peace from these activities, which really supports my well-being, but

that's just me. For you, it might be reading, yoga or meeting a friend.

4. Get a really good accountant. Only work with accountants who come highly recommended. It will save you valuable time and money in the long run.

5. Build a positive culture for your organisation from day one. This feeds into your ethics and your branding as a business – whether you plan on going solo or building a company with employees, it all starts with you. Start as you mean to go on.

6. Value your business partnerships, business associates and colleagues at all times. Nurturing them is crucial from both a moral point of view, but it also benefits you and your business. If you look after your relationships, they will support you to look after your business, which is great, because it can get very lonely out there!

7. I've said it before, and I'll say it again. And as I mentioned earlier in the book it's a cliché, but if you want to scale your business, it's very difficult if you are actually working in the business. It's far more productive to work on the business. Not everybody wants to scale and that's also fine; you may love what you do and want to be involved in the delivery of the service at all levels. Don't be afraid to outsource things though, such as your website, marketing and accounting. So, I'll say again – use trusted recommendations.

8. No matter how big or how successful your business gets, keep your head. Surround yourself with people who are supportive and believe in you, but also people who are honest. Sometimes you need people to tell you how it is. Success, as well as failure, can be temporary, so never forget where you came from and who supported you to get there.

9. Stay true to yourself. Be authentic and remember what's important to you in life and in your business. Why did you come into the care sector in the first place?

10. Tony Robinson OBE told me that you need three things to succeed in business: someone who is fantastic with finances, someone who is great operationally and someone amazing at marketing. Not many people can do all three. At some point, you may need help!

Good luck and enjoy the adventure of being a care entrepreneur!

Big Ian visiting me in Scarborough

My family

My wife Emma and I at a Hollywood Themed 'Apart' Charity Ball

TESTIMONIALS FOR CARE IMPROVEMENT ASSOCIATES

"The basis of any successful care business is high quality provision and customer and colleague engagement. At Bluebird Care, we are exceptionally proud of the quality of the services we provide; in fact, 2019 saw a 7G% uplift in the number of Bluebird Care businesses achieving the highest regulatory ratings.

Working with Sam and the team at CIA provides our owners and their operational teams access to evidenced-based guidance, enabling them to take their quality ambitions to the next level.

We're proud to be working with CIA and look forward to developing the relationship further over the coming months and years."

– Leading national home care franchise group, Bluebird Care.

"Cera are committed to excellence in care quality, so naturally, we are delighted to be working with CIA. Our shared vision for improving care across the nation has been a key driver for the ease and scale at which we have been able to work together.

The team have shown real dedication and set us up for success right from the start, and we are excited to see what we can achieve with their support."

– Leading national home care provider, Cera

"We engaged Care Improvement Associates Ltd on a bespoke assignment to enhance our management insight from an external and more objective angle and perspective.

We were Delighted with both the service and support received from the head office at CIA, as well as the professional consultant assigned to the project.

We would highly recommend CIA's services and would certainly commission their services again in future, should the need arise."

– Mike Padgham, Chairman of Independent Care Group (ICG)

"It was our pleasure to have the CIA 'Mock Inspection Team' with us – the two days went extremely well and they both confirmed the areas of improvement we expected, and it was reassuring to know that our own identified priorities were accurate.

The insight they were both able to give, and the ideas and suggestions were extremely useful and the team were left feeling very inspired."

– Jamie Anderson, CEO Age UK (Wirral)

"Voyage Care are committed to the provision of outstanding care and support for every person we support. We are proud to have a proven track record for delivering support that is innovative, high quality and responsive. In order to enable attainment of positive outcomes for people, we ensure that all our care and support specialisms are underpinned by nationally recognised evidence and best practice.

Voyage Care are delighted to have engaged Care Improvement Associates Ltd to support us with the continued development of our sector-leading specialisms. CIA bring independence, professionalism and a critical eye to the development of new processes and specialisms, which absolutely supports delivery of our strategy."

– Amanda Griffiths,
Quality Director at Voyage Care

For more testimonials, visit our website at
www.theciagroup.co.uk

Printed in Great Britain
by Amazon

19133351R00051